Praise for *Camouflage of Noise and Silence*

In Camouflage of Noise and Silence, Barry DeCarli balances light and dark, pleasure and pain, and joy and sorrow with masterful strokes. DeCarli anchors his layered poems in the real world of pawn shops, hospitals, Thanksgiving dinner, childhood homes, and winter gardens where his words offer simple truth and humor against the backdrop of long-ago dreams, family bonds, and recurrent memories: "yet we fail / to hear the words / of those closest to us / or what they mean / the daily signals we do not receive / filtered out by the white noise of routine." His meditations on life's choices and taking loved ones for granted are universal, as are his poems about the inevitability of aging: "we irritate like nettles / we get under the skin / like poison oak or ivy / in the closed quarters of friendship / and family / we become indiscriminate even / to those we love." DeCarli succeeds in crafting a deeply personal collection of poems that connects and engages—isn't this everything we want great poetry to achieve?

Alice Osborn, author of Heroes without Capes

I find Barry DeCarli's Camouflage of Noise and Silence intriguing and in the same breath unsettling. Intriguing because he presents us with philosophical questions and unsettling because we are then faced with answering them on our own. DeCarli is a brilliant wordsmith and has given me a new appreciation for poetry. I adore "a candled soul" where he offers, "maybe someone / can find a way in / carrying scales and light / to weigh, and to candle / even your embryonic dreams / your age-old regrets…" This is most certainly a collection of poems for a logophile, but I think even more so for someone who is yet to appreciate well-crafted work.

Katie Thompson, award winning New Zealand singer / songwriter,
opened for Elton John in his Dunedin NZ concert

Camouflage
of Noise
and
Silence

Camouflage
of Noise
and
Silence

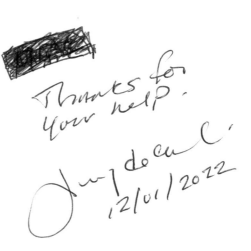

poems by
Barry DeCarli

First Edition

Cover design: Artwork/photo by Barry DeCarli
Comments/inquiries to: onsouthstreetpress@gmail.com
barrydecarlipoetry.com

an Off The Common Book
Amherst & Florence, Massachusetts

ISBN 978-1-951928-13-1

Also by Barry DeCarli

Almost 1979
Of Sun and Rain 1972

For Deborah Rooney DeCarli,
my wife and best friend.

"Be patient toward all that is unsolved in your heart and try to love the questions themselves, like locked rooms and like books that are now written in a very foreign tongue. Do not now seek the answers, which cannot be given you because you would not be able to live them. And the point is, to live everything. Live the questions now. Perhaps you will then gradually, without noticing it, live along some distant day into the answer."

Rainer Maria Rilke

Contents

listening

Arecibo eavesdropping
on the universe
tilting at windmills
concentrating, listening
this giant receiver catching sounds
or silence from an endless sky

yet we fail
to hear the words
of those closest to us
or misunderstand what they mean
the daily signals we do not receive
filtered out by the white noise of routine

so many pins dropping
conversations pending

how many messages
strained by light years
of cosmic noise
or silent black holes
are lost
even when the willingness
to hear is strong
a plea can ricochet
off surfaces unseen
garbled by distances
now impossible to cross
still we press our drinking glass
against the wall of the universe
disappointed, yet
relieved at the silence

awaiting a message
we seem
so unprepared to receive
searching for a sign
a sound of life
beyond the walls
of our own atmosphere

so we'll know that seven billion of us
are not alone

the rose and the raspberry

we grow thorns
like the rose
and the raspberry
to keep us from slipping
to protect us
from our enemies
how similar we are
to the barbed plants
we tend
the gardens we neglect

we irritate like nettles
we get under the skin
like poison oak or ivy
in the closed quarters of friendship
and family
we become indiscriminate even
to those we love

sometimes we are
passive partners
the stoic sentries
standing against a storm
a season
awaiting the dormant demands to come
our fear fertile
with exaggeration or excuse
prepared to break off
but not to bend

willing to squander
history and evolution
for our prickly pride
taking what beauty we can
while leaving behind
the waste of
our
reckless

pruning

my muse, his devils

wanting to pour poetry
from a bottle
of Pinot Grigio
to uncork the perfect pairing of
words and emotion
in an untitled document
trying to escape the collision
of headache and hope with
the right metaphor
stoking my muse there in the wine
my poem scrapes against the easiness
of inkjet black on white

my father stood unsteadily
the car was his medium
driven with a practiced recklessness
he sought to slake a more primal thirst
trying to wash away his devils
as the bourbon burned his throat
then softly drenched
his drought of dreams
for a while he found forgiveness
fulfillment there in the bottle
his Oldsmobile keyed with barbed wire
while taking out the farmer's fence
there was nothing easy about his poetry
of rubber and speed
steel and noise

break a leg

so many disguises
overflowing from
the steamer trunks
of our lives

we are bit players
not stars
in our own play
emerging from our dressing rooms
always in costume
make-up applied

staying in character
to protect who
we think
we ought to be
or to hide who
we know we are

so much energy
wasted masking
our true face
as the magnificence
of our souls
masquerades
behind the rouge

obscuring
promise
creation and risk
but mostly denying
the possibility
of failure

year after year
we rehearse
the vague lines
of small talk
to no one who
could care

while refusing
to allow
even an ad lib
or an inkling
of our own depth

to break the surface

similar wars

another war ending
more guilty feelings for not
being able to pick up a gun
or grenade
or hear a fellow soldier's dying wish
to carry a letter home

some freedom of speech lost here

where that war
had more protest than this one
we might have put a daisy
in a gun barrel
and said "make love, not war"
or as easily scorned the soldier

surely the feelings are different now

my reluctance hardly balances
your willingness
my comfort weighs lightly
on your sacrifice
my desire for self-preservation
is too thin a veil to obscure your courage
my inability to know what I might die for
can not diminish your steadfast belief
that you were doing the right thing
yet, at the end, I am here alive
and you are number 4,556
on the list of those lost to memory

who can say thank you now
and have it mean anything
to your family, to anyone

conscripted, enlisted, dodged
or the luck of a high lottery number
does it matter whether this war
was any more necessary than that war
can it matter now

if your death or my life was in vain

resurrection

what does await
where standing stones exercise
their stillness
their silence
in this garden
where graves lay burdened
by a weight of soil
and sorrow

what could lift the concrete lid
that encases and keeps
maybe the steel teeth of a backhoe
but not the feeble equipment of remembrance
not the absent and elusive soul

what does await
when resurrection will not come
when memory too
lapses and dies
can exhumation bring anything
but disturbance
disappointment

and reburial

church

where is your church?
mine is in the medieval hill towns
of Pienza and Montepulciano
along the quiet dusky
cobbled paths on the limestone ridge

tasting its namesake wines
marveling
in amazement
looking up to the risky parapets
the muted bell towers at times
still heralding the misery
and the joy from here
to Montalcino

my church catches the sunset
and the shadows
through the stone gate
at Monteriggioni
and cools the Tuscan piazza
below the city walls

it is in a museum
where paintings of Caravaggio and
Michelangelo hang frozen in Florentine time
forever at home with the Medicis
so near Savonarola's bonfire of the arts
(and then of his own flesh)

where truth and beauty arise from the ashes

beyond buildings and places
shadows and sunsets
mine is where our souls meet
recognizing
understanding
and knowing

where we feel
see and hear true genius
or in the unlikely reconciliation of adversaries
where making one of opposites
light and dark
hate and love
death and life

brings tears to my eyes

missed message

the excess of time becomes
too little to waste
while the pain grows
and lasts
even as cells turn brittle
broken
when learning lacks memory

no wonder we miss
the sign
pulsing inside our eyelids
the message cannot break through
our diaphragm of perception
that some forgetful god is unable
to shape an answer other than

no

memory

it might have been disappointment that
gave flight
to that lava hot burner
across the cold kitchen
or anger
but it was my mother
who stood her ground there
by the stove
handle in hand

as the nearly molten discus crash landed
short of its mark
at my father's unsteady feet

its circle brand smoking itself
into worn linoleum
acrid uncertainty
hanging in the air

a half century later
though the house may be cinders
caved into its foundation
the taste of burnt linseed oil
smoldering cork and
the fear of an uncertain future
still remain

august afternoon

august leaves rustled
like some misbegotten ritual,
a funeral day
slow and quiet,
sad and long.

rooms smelled of musty furniture.
a shade caught the breeze
then bumped against the sash.
dust particles floated
disturbed
in a faint shaft of light.

small voices
of children
squeezed through the screen,
a filtered background for the stillness,
this suspended movement.

beyond the murmuring
a whisper from the window,

try to get some sleep,
your dreams are on their way.

taking steps in a stranger's shoes

wondering whose shoes caked
with pain or sorrow
she must lace up tomorrow
where that mile will take her

the burden is hers to carry
millstone or milestone
albatross or golden fleece

a heavy talisman that does not
ward off but accepts
the anguish, the dread
of someone's sadness
even a stranger's feelings
who will never know

what makes her care
what carries her forward

blessing or curse
gravity or grace

the price of memories

what outside influence
intrudes upon us stealthily
stealing our breath like carbon monoxide
letting us do something we don't want to
explain

as the soaring price of
precious metals seeped into our consciousness
heirlooms have found their way
reversing the gold rush
to pawn shops
coin dealers
hotel lobbies
instead of into jewelry boxes
dresser drawers of nieces
or nephews

no dust or danger
no pack horse or partner
searching for Sutter's Mill
instead a paved strip-mall parking lot
with a sandwich bag of class rings, lockets, chains
the remains, the props of the past
the stuff of personal history
more than gold traded but

less than a scruple or a grain
the memories weigh easy
on the digital scale
the tipping point

some logic that someone else

will just stake their claim

after we're gone

afterwards

scientists say
matter
or energy
can't be created or destroyed
only conserved

or changed
is there a physics
a chemistry of memory
a weight or worth
to some spiritual commodity
when remembered

but when it's
irretrievable
unknown
forgotten by all

is it nothing then
or matter stored for another time
is there more of it
after sharing
can it change in the telling
the turn of the tale

after words
does memory matter
waiting to be retrieved
there in the soil

beneath the stone and grass

Obsidian revelation

have you ever looked
too closely
at your own reflection
have you ever
wished that you didn't
know the imperfections

do you remember
finding out
that the magic you witnessed
was nothing
but an illusion
smoke and mirrors
that had sucked you in

was it better not knowing
that a charade could hurt
especially when you
played the scene with your head
or your heart as props

sometimes
reality carries
its hidden liability
behind a shield of naivety
to protect us
from the staggering wounds
of the truth

but when the mirror's smoky surface
exposes you
revealing your flaws

can you ever un-see its revelation

the masters

how they stumbled
upon their insight
conjured the words
to a common language
what amazing things they imagined
created
invented
as they paired the pigments
mined the marble
and the metaphor

how did they uncover the riches
with so little history
behind them
the benefit of so few volumes
no Internet
to leave us with Alighieri's *Divine Comedy*
Michelangelo's *Pieta*
DaVinci's *The Last Supper*

what idea compelled them to sacrifice
their lives to create a masterpiece
what desire pulled them forward
in poverty
in desperation to leave us
with the priceless treasures
of their blood
their sweat
the everlasting vision of their dreams

with all our burgeoning access to information
our gluttony for resources
our unbridled enthusiasm for change
for wealth
for comfort

what will we leave

kaleidoscope

better obscurity
than the scrutiny
of examining eyes
this kaleidoscope of our own
broken pieces held
up to the light

some may see beauty
some pain and waste
from the rainbow of color
and jagged edges

tumbling as we turn
to the next catastrophe
or epiphany
the mirrored hall of scattered
dreams, tattered triumphs

the spare glory days
conjured with the turn
of a hand illuminating
the bits and beads
the shards of yesterday
the loose ends

the arbitrary patterns
of bliss and blunder roll
to reflect our tunnel vision until
the fractured light shows us
the mismatched fragments

wedded and welded
by shade and color
some sharp edges saltwater sanded
to a sea glass satin
always the same
yet ever-changing

still we turn the lens
to view our own evolution
in this prism of broken pieces
and mirrored jagged beauty
looking up once more
to find the light
we wonder if it's worth
another turn

malediction

who knows where
something will go
the outcome
of words spoken
sincerely
angrily

intention conjured like a curse

when a sorry joke
is lost in the satire
then taken seriously
when misunderstanding
is the only understanding

when a nagging suspicion
that an apology
might be in order
though the need of it
couldn't seem further from

the truth

the meaning
or just the memory of something said
can hang there

forever

held by some ghost of semantics
phobia or fear
still bouncing
    between
the lines

waking

the brightening fringe of morning
a tranquil tinge of soft white
between the curtains
the gentle hand of daybreak
a symphony of dewdrops
the lament of a waking dove

dandelions in a yellow yawn
sister of dusk
daughter of dark
mother of morning

dawn

truth

the truth may come
hopefully
cascading sunlight overwhelming
the drenched meadow
vindication
that bearing the storm
was worth its burden
for this exclamation of misty color

or truth may come more blatantly
like a scalding bath
sloughing
off the skin of lies
burning to the bone
exploding marrow
in the sanguine spatter

of surprise

right to farm

the rooster crows unpredictably
morning and afternoon
sunrise to sunset
sometimes after

farm equipment for planting
for harvesting forms two rust-pocked rows
of red, green and white
lettered Farmall, John Deere, Massey-Ferguson
even one grey Ford
faded, quiet and waiting

the herd of Holsteins
loaded last week in rattling metal trailers
for a panicked ride to some industrial dairy
the driver unacquainted with the work
of Temple Grandin

there is no market for the rooster
or his incessant hollering
but still no time to sleep
for this 4th generation farmer
finally idle in the hours before dawn
turning over fields in his mind
imagining the end of
that mocking wake-up call
as the ax slams down

with the finality of the auctioneer's gavel

hunger pangs

sometimes
we get a taste
of tomorrow
a tease on the tongue
but we are afraid
to bite into it
to swallow
to savor something
we just hope for

other times
the flavor of yesterday
remains
long past its ripeness
when we should know
to spit it out
and move on

but most times
we drink in the tasteless
moments of today
washing down
our hope for the future
while the dreams of our past

still linger on our lips

a candled soul

would you welcome
a microscopic look at your own essence
someone peering through a magnifying lens
to discover what's there
and what isn't

someone who would unwrap your secrets
where your words are only wishes
where your thoughts barely hint
but don't reveal
as they skim the surface

yielding no more than a glimmer in your eye

maybe someone
can find a way in
carrying scales and light
to weigh and to candle
even your embryonic dreams
your age-old regrets

someone who can see through your tempered skin
past your veins, muscle and bone
to view just how you balance
what you don't say with what you will
to glimpse your soul

what if that revelation is
not a violation of your own private shell

but a release

surrender

some friends suffer
in the silence
of a deafening distance
while sensing a closeness
of memory
across the uninterrupted expanse
between hope and

the horizon
they stand still
staring at yesterday
the sentinels of recollection
scan the vastness as memories
ricochet off the walls
of what was

often the silence and distance
gain the strength of time
the years adding up
defeat a desire to reconnect

while raising the white flag
above the rutted path
of least resistance

crazing

don't be afraid
to become more
radical
more misunderstood
to show your underside
that reveals some crazing
a rough edge
an uncultured moment

but prepare
to be estranged
for lesser infractions
shunned after some cruel unmasking
as others serve up
their own emotional bankruptcy

to counter your revelation
your imperfection

their fear

dignity

for Debbie's father, John Rooney

he began reaching out
behind him
to his left side
knowing someone was there to take his hand
sensing some seriousness
as high flow oxygen hissed
in his chapped nostrils

then
the startling realization
I have no clothes here
I am not going home

his left hand moved toward his forehead
we thought he was in pain
and called for a nurse

but, maybe he was just trying to remember
struggling to pull just one
more memory out
a lucid argument that would allow him to live
a little while longer

the morphine delivered
a dreamy comfort
as the demands of his body
diminished one by one

when finally
the promise of his soul
let him go…

canned memory

I've never liked eating raw, fleshy clams
that you let slide down your throat
smooth and slippery from their butter bath
their texture or lack of it
urgently signals my gag response
so opposite of a buttered biscuit
or corn-on-the-cob dripping and salted
popping the sweet kernels with my teeth

I can still picture my mother
at the white enamel stove
heating ravioli over the kerosene flame
the blackened steel frying pan releasing
familiar aromas, but none of basil, garlic or olive oil
pine nuts or parmesan
al dente was a language not spoken
yet I remember my mouth watering
ready to slide those steaming morsels from Chef Boyardee
down my throat like clams on the half-shell

destiny

we carry the clue
to the mystery of tomorrow
coming and going

at times
we are conscious creators
of destiny
planning and dreaming

we write the riddle
we try to solve
hoping and guessing

yet
we are still plagued
by the uncertainty
of it all

choosing and waiting

refugees

but for the tears
a small boy may shed
his childhood has been torn from him
discarded on the tracks
a bloodied rag left behind
another past drying up
blowing across the oiled ties

scorpions dance over the cooling grey stones
he watches as if they are toys
he cannot have
his mother's glimmering eyes hold
the idea of home
to light the path ahead
through the dark cruel shadows

even as the razor wire slices deep
as terror tempers her hope
she does not let go of his hand

mourning

when someone dies
maybe a new black hole opens
somewhere
in the universe
a place where the soul
can find respite in its great journey forward
beyond our understanding
out of sight of our grief
leaving behind the sounds of our sorrow

but what of our private tears
the sorrow we do not share
at a gravesite vigil
or while reading an obituary
as we mourn a stranger
like those we knew
what of the sobs no one hears
who can fathom their meaning

does a black hole open
to accept those too

baptised

imagine the man o'war sting
of holy water
as an infant
already fearful
of the hand of God
cries out
as the dripping finger inscribes a cross
on her fragile forehead

crucifixed

touched and tinctured
the promise of a life
everlasting
tempered by words
that only wish
she will have a long life

then the thundering order
of a prayer
intoned
compels her unaware
into Christianity

ring less true

there's more to truth
than just right words,
and so much less
to lies.
yet, a lie
seems the stronger
of the two,
as truth so often dies.
when disbelief
can cloud the eyes,
there's little
we can do
but hang on to some wispy hope
that the lie will ring less true.

no teaser

called out
for teasing with my words
a faker fashioning phrases
to lure a trusting mind
into my poetic snare

I'd rather be
a magician pulling a thesaurus
out of a hat

a dreamer catching a falling star
holding its rhyme
in a Mason jar

a lamplighter reaching
up to light a circle
of night air
a patch of dark ground
a way home

but not a teaser
keeping a secret
or trying to deceive
with my images that anyone may see

my metaphors as deep as a mirror...

the expense of speech

just sit quietly
nodding

don't talk
politics
religion
welfare with family
in other words
no hard feelings
to keep other feelings

from exploding into estrangement

is blood really thicker
than meaning
than the essence of someone's soul

leave yourself at the door
all offense
insult
agreement
distilled into small talk about weather
nieces
nephews

Red Sox & Yankees

well, maybe
leave them at the door
too

imagine

for Yukako Sorai

could I
too imagine the stars
as I rolled this
fiber form
in the palm
of my hand

more than just
black and white
felt
she imagined
but a small piece
of the night
sky

could she
too conjure
a piece of the universe
our own Earth

for us to hold close
with both hands
to share
to shelter
to keep safe

noise

bulldozer blade bullying rocks
out of hard-packed ground
grinding a fresh surface
a cacophony of stone against steel
blade against boulder
restlessness against rock
boulders tumbling across
a dented tailgate
the dull groan of stone against dirt
echoing off water and sky
the chalky muted growl of rock
against rock

what if these sounds could form a foundation
a place to stand
to hold back the next mudslide
the next descent
what if this noise alone could deliver sanctuary
to protect us
decibel by decibel
from the silence we're afraid to hear

would we still block our ears

polarization

we do share
a common ground
though sometimes we
can't see the place
where we could meet
in the space
between
our houses
between our bodies
however distant
or in the pause
between our words
where we consider
intent and motive

where wedded to
our willingness
to find grace
we may find an
understanding of give and take

but will intellect or ignorance
force us apart
until we no longer stand
but instead lie under
the ground that will be
so common to all of us

revolution

are we too reticent
for revolution
political or otherwise

even free of the American Dream
comfort does not escape us
chaos reassures no one
but the anarchist and
the opportunist

our fear of unleashing a beast
even briefly
holds us in check
wondering
could that beast be our burden
as well as our savior

still we settle
into our place by the warm fire
as the wolves of change begin
to whimper impatiently somewhere
off in the distance

our fear of the worst
may keep us
from embracing the best
even as the ramparts begin to tumble down
will we once again choose the monster we know
but cannot tame

desperation

must there
be a gaping wound
flowing with blood
must our cheeks be streaked with crying
must we stagger
and fall
then must we crawl
before someone reaches out
before our words are heard
before it is too late
how obvious must the truth be
how blatant the wrong
when what is apparent
is
lost
in
the
lie
we all become victims
of the desperation
we seek to ignore
for in making beggars of the desperate
we become the ones
truly in need…

what we wish for

as it turns out
we were no longer
knights
in our camouflaged armor
we did not glisten
we did not light the way

we killed the tyrants
to free the psychopaths

never once realizing
who actually held the world
together
we cut off the strong arm
toppled a statue
to unleash this wild beast
of freedom
that today threatens
to tear our world apart

shingles

waking
to a new monster
in the morning mirror

whose face is this

what grotesque mask
what masquerade makes over
a face

swollen above and
below the blurred gauze
of eyesight
wincing
the weighted eyelid
drooping

once here
there's no going back
or escaping this
childhood revenge

long dormant
now stirring just under
the skin
tickling at first
a teasing feather unseen
or tiny spiders scurrying
to get out
silently trekking from
spine to forehead

the pharmaceutical cocktail
of acyclovir, acetaminophen
and erythromycin
offers up a mixture of hope
and headache
healing and humility
while unbalanced pain
punctuates this withdrawal from sight
another day inside as
the Trojan Horse of

chicken pox
offers up the blistering head
of vanity
to the looking glass

hidden

parts of life
exist in the shadow
of truth
of openness
there in the fog of evening
a small secret lies
an un-daring deception concealed
beneath the camouflage of silence
the cloud of sorrow

the untelling of past lives
stifles the need to share that
lingers like sweat's moisture
cooling the surface of silence

unrepeated stories
fleeing memory
atrophied
lost in the reluctance
to ration more than a hint

parts of life dying off
each melancholic year
memories unable to lift themselves
out of the past

broken

maybe
some mistakes can't be fixed
the hope for forgiveness
is not strong enough
to lift the weight of apology
at our feet
there can be no making amends
even among family
or friends

opening wounds comes easier
than closing them
the scars won't take us back
to any safe place we knew
no bridge can take us across the divide

anger and embarrassment
hurt and hubris
become the building blocks
of the wall we engineer
with the simmering energy of emotion

wanting to stop the pain
with our mortar of stubborn silence
our pride sets each stone

the last word

nonna and old-world Italy
faced the pop, hip-hop teenage girl today
but the battle became no war

the words from nona's mouth
were not wrinkled like her face
as they smoothly took aim
at the goose-bumped skin
of the girl nearly coming of age

cover yourself up!

the command
broke the silence and
stopped the shivers
the reaction was not textbook
as the pop, hip-hop teenage girl
quickly wrapped herself in a beach towel
and walked away without a smirk
no rolled eyes
or a word

suggesting that her string bikini
on this day
was no match
for nonna's babushka

hail mary

so little chance
not a prayer
for redemption
for victory
still we try
we whisper
our not-so-humble plea

but so little happens
as most hail marys
are dropped
or bounce
out of bounds

others are intercepted by silence
like so many prayers
tossed up
only to land in disappointment

yet when one is received
caught and held close
then raised high
amidst the raucous revelry
of disbelief
our arrogance proclaims a miracle

human history

what of all the missing
and missed moments
the magnitude
the magnificence
even the mediocrity
of all the memories
lost to time

who would feel compelled
to catalog them all
who would be willing to try to remember
to recount each thought
that each human being
had considered in a lifetime

is there enough
memory in the cloud
for billions of sighs and whispers
dreams and schemes
secrets, songs and sonnets
so much lost to the silent history
that death and indifference leave
the ramblings and ravings
longing and yearning

what of the millions
who waited for an invitation
a subpoena that did not come
never asked to bear witness
to their own lives
what they had seen
and said
what was important
what drew their tears
their laughter
will no one be able to tell their story
will nothing chronicle that they ever lived

would anyone know what lies beneath
the ragged wooden cross, the crumbling cairn of stones
how much could be chiseled

onto a headstone
words that so few would ever read
cemeteries holding so much cold hard truth

what of our failure to offer even a penny for their thoughts

hope

(after the Boston Marathon bombing)

can it survive
where is it
in the deaths
of Martin Richard
Krystle Campbell
Lu Lingzi

where is it
among the twisted
torn and broken limbs
the riddled bodies
the amputations

in the aftermath
of tragedy
in the bloodied fingers
and knees
the held hands

can it be found
in the resounding anthem
at a hockey game
in the act of a new Pope
cleansing and kissing
the feet of men, women
and Muslims

is it in a million prayers
sent out
across a violent sky
to the imagined
face of god
and in a Neil Diamond song
or in a YouTube video
of a dancing queen

is it found
in other countries
where bomb blasts
are as ordinary

as thunder
and hunger
where resignation
will not bring peace

can it be found

sometimes
in the wrong
places
in the midst of carnage
and crying
blood and glass

after the unfathomable loss
shock and senselessness
will we pick the bones
of grief
to find it

there

the meaning

keep a pen and notebook
next to the nightstand of your life
be ready to record
the scent of emotion
a fleeting idea
the tears of trees
an inkling of a dream
the longing whisper of leaves
the subtle song of the sky
the sweet promise of dawn
the savory taste of evening

scribble down
some crazy thought

milk the darkness
squeeze the diary of your mind
for just a bit of sense
to find some sequence
of wonder and worry
laughter and love
truth and tale

observe something
or anything
below the surface you've only been scraping
so you can write down
the part you remember
some vestige of hope
the glimmer of a greater or
a lesser meaning

so someone else might see

heritage

for my father, Antonio P. DeCarli and a boy he never knew, Bentley Davis Seifer

questions of potential
haunt the mourners of this boy
Snowflake Bentley's namesake
could he have produced paintings
that might hang in the museum of art
or design an airport internationale
a launch pad to the milky way
who knows, could he have hit 800 home runs
after all, he was so much younger than Shelley
when the water pulled him under

what about such prolific possibility
Shakespeare
Lennon and McCartney
Solzhenitsyn
Marco Polo or Stephen Hawking
why question genius
while we hold the proof in our hands
maybe, to let us off the hook
so we could say
no one could have done all that

what could my father have done
had life been different
had his desire raged at another god
had his muse spoken with more promise
but he did not waste his life being who he was
he did what he could
no manuscripts, no treatise to show his wisdom
no invention to ease our burden
no compound to ease our pain
no perfect poem

(just three good sons)

still
here we are
this soup of genetics
different hopes, fears
and dreams
he left behind

lives lived with his imprint on our souls

that is no small thing

once

no camera
to capture this moon
settling into grey
from a fading layer of
purple turning pink
beneath such baby blue
while from behind
the sun
is lighting mountaintops
to reflect another age

imagine
other eyes seeing this
5,000 years ago
with no way to relate the beauty
before them
other than to gasp
before it disappeared

yet, we are here
because they survived that winter with
fire only in their hearts
they witnessed this cold stark grandeur
and passed it on through eons of time
to blaze into our DNA
the genetic photograph
that lets us take in the splendor
unfolding today
across this winter sky

pareidolia

the face of Christ on
a piece toast
some plaster in Pittsburgh
a pancake at the Cowgirl Cafe
on the Shroud of Turin
looking as much like Charles Manson
or Che Guevara
as Jesus

Mother Mary appearing
between hospital window panes
near Boston
or on a tree trunk
in Iowa

religious Rorschachs
only perceived by some
mocked by others
with a clearer vision
or none at all

camera ready
a few search for a sign
look for hope
in a bowl of corn flakes

most laugh at the phenomenon
this prophecy
whose medium might be mold,
misty moisture or
burning bread

but others
not blinded
by impossibility
might see a miracle
dancing in their heads

a bridge

there are things
to reconcile
to redeem
to reclaim
and to lose

the past is racing
to overcome
its own memory
surging recollection
daring today

reach back, reach back

but there are things
to risk
and reasons not to

to stay here today

is each step we take
a question or an answer
is the bridge to burn
or to cross

the life we spend is on the span
are we crossing
or going back

Camouflage of Noise and Silence is Barry DeCarli's third book of poems. His first collection, *Of Sun and Rain*, was published in 1972. *Almost*, his second collection, came out in 1979. Over the years his poems have appeared in *This Singing World (Hartford Courant)*, *The Contemporary (CCSU)*, *Poetry from Hartford* and *The Lake Champlain Maritime Museum Newsletter*, and more recently online in *The Ekphrastic Review* and *The Poetry Vending Machine Project (Attack Bear Press)*. DeCarli earned degrees from Central Connecticut State University (BA) and the University of Vermont (M. Ed). He retired in 2010 after 22 years as a high school special education teacher in Middlebury, VT. In his spare time, Barry runs, reads, likes to travel and buys & sells eclectic old things on eBay. Barry and his wife, Debbie, live in western Massachusetts with their English Setter, Sandie.